NOTTI...

A MISCELLANY

Compiled by Julia Skinner

With particular reference to the work of
Martin Andrew and Douglas Whitworth

THE FRANCIS FRITH COLLECTION

www.francisfrith.com

First published in the United Kingdom in 2010 by The Francis Frith Collection®

This edition published exclusively for Bradwell Books in 2013
For trade enquiries see: www.bradwellbooks.com or tel: 0800 834 920
978-1-84589-519-8

British Library Cataloguing in Publication Data

Did You Know? Nottinghamshire - A Miscellany
Compiled by Julia Skinner
With particular reference to the work of Martin Andrew and Douglas Whitworth

The Francis Frith Collection
6 Oakley Business Park,
Wylye Road, Dinton,
Wiltshire SP3 5EU
Tel: +44 (0) 1722 716 376
Email: info@francisfrith.co.uk
www.francisfrith.com

Printed and bound in Malaysia
Contains material sourced from responsibly managed forests

Front Cover: **NOTTINGHAM, THE CASTLE GATEHOUSE 1890** 22843p

The colour-tinting is for illustrative purposes only, and is not intended to be historically accurate

CONTENTS

INTRODUCTION

Nottinghamshire assumed much of its present character in the 18th century, when Enclosure Acts divided up the open fields of the villages into neat hawthorn-hedged small fields, and industry arrived, particularly around Nottingham itself, which began to grow quickly. Cotton mills and machine-lace factories supplanted the home-workers' hand looms, stocking-frames and lace bobbins, and the mechanisation of industry and deep coal-mining transformed parts of the county.

Some of the photographs in this book show Nottinghamshire in the 1940s, 1950s and 1960s. This was a time when the coal mines still functioned all along the west of the county, and huge coal-fired power stations were built along the River Trent, supplied with coal from the Nottinghamshire coalfield by barge and railway. This was a time (before Dr Beeching's drastic cuts of the 1960s) when branch railways could take you to virtually every village, and when Gresley's great steam locomotives hauled the Flying Scotsman and other expresses along the east coast main line of the London and North Eastern Region (LNER), passing through Newark and Retford on their way to Doncaster and the north.

One of the biggest changes for Nottinghamshire in recent times was the closure in the 1980s of virtually all the coal mines along the west side of the county, including Babbington, Arnold and Clifton collieries in the environs of Nottingham, Brinsley Pit near Eastwood, and Costhorpe near Langold. The Nottinghamshire mines initially came through unscathed during the first wave of closures after the miners' strike during Margaret Thatcher's premiership, but they could not outface the conversion of the River Trent power stations to gas.

**OLLERTON, THORESBY HALL
THE ROBIN HOOD STATUE c1955** O131039

NOTTINGHAMSHIRE DIALECT WORDS AND PHRASES

'A ya masht miduck?' - Have you made a pot of tea?

'Clemmed' - can mean either very cold, or very hungry.

'Corsey' - pavement.

'Derby road' - cold, as in **'It's Derby road',** it's a bit cold.

'Jitty' - an alleyway between houses.

'Kaled' - delayed, held up.

'Laruped' - covered with, as in 'laruped in mud'.

'Mardy' - moody, crying, whingeing, as in 'a mardy child'.

'Rammel' - rubble, rubbish.

'Snap' - food taken to eat at work. **'Snap tin'** - the food container.

'Throng' or **'thronged'** - very busy, as in **'The town was throng today'**.

SOUTHWELL, CARRIAGE IN KING STREET 1920 69472x

HAUNTED NOTTINGHAMSHIRE

It was at Nottingham Castle that the young King Edward III trapped his mother, Queen Isabella, with her lover, Roger Mortimer, and created the legend of Mortimer's hole. This was said to be a cave leading from the cellars of Ye Olde Trip to Jerusalem Inn to the castle, through which Edward III is reputed to have crept to capture Mortimer, who was later put to death. Mortimer's ghost is said to haunt the cave.

Strange happenings have been reported at Wollaton Hall near Nottingham. Attendants at the Hall have felt the temperature suddenly drop, or been aware of a hostile presence, often accompanied by the sound of a door slamming, footsteps, creaking floorboards and groans, particularly in Room 19, now used as an exhibition area. Investigations found that Room 19 was where Lady Middleton was confined in her later years, in great pain after an accident in which she fell down some stairs. The area outside the Hall also seems to be haunted – strange lights have been seen around the dovecote and stable yard, and a ghostly woman walking her dog has been seen near the lake.

The ghost of a young woman called Elizabeth Sheppard is said to haunt Harlow Wood, near Mansfield, around the spot where she was murdered in 1817 by a scissor-grinder, Charles Rotherham, who attacked her with a wooden stake whilst she was making her way to Mansfield to seek work. Rotherham was apprehended a few days later when he tried to sell Elizabeth's shoes in an inn at Redhill, and was hanged at Nottingham. There is a memorial stone to Elizabeth on the A60, about half a mile north of the junction with the B6020 Kirkby road, and her ghost is said to appear whenever the stone is moved.

Newstead Abbey is said to be haunted by several ghosts, including a Black Friar whose appearances always herald disaster – the poet Lord Byron, whose home Newstead Abbey was, claimed to have seen this ghost before embarking on his ill-fated marriage to Annabella Millbank in 1815.

MANSFIELD, CHURCH STREET 1949 M184007

NOTTINGHAMSHIRE MISCELLANY

Nottinghamshire is a county steeped in history, and is often called 'Robin Hood Country'. It is not known for sure whether Robin Hood ever really existed – the Robin Hood of legend may be an amalgam of several historical figures – but in the later Middle Ages Nottinghamshire became the location for stories of this outlaw who stole from the rich and gave to the poor, with various real places and people added to the tales, such as Sherwood Forest where the Merry Men lived, Edwinstowe where legend says that Robin married Maid Marian, and, of course, the Sheriff of Nottingham and Nottingham Castle. Nottinghamshire now trades on all this with a Robin Hood Festival in Sherwood Forest and the Robin Hood Pageant at Nottingham Castle, as well as the Robin Hood Way long-distance footpath.

OLLERTON, SHERWOOD FOREST c1955 O131014

Sherwood Forest once covered over 100,000 acres between Nottingham and Worksop. As early as the 10th century, this vast tract of wooded landscape was known as 'sher wood', meaning 'the wood belonging to the county, or shire', and by the 12th century it was a royal forest subject to its own Forest Law. The view shown in photograph O131014 (above) is in the Sherwood Forest Country Park, an area of 450 acres with many of the best surviving ancient oak trees amid silver birch, younger oaks and bracken. Visitors may also catch glimpse here of fallow deer, and even roe and red deer.

At the heart of the Sherwood Forest Country Park is the famous Major Oak, about half a mile west of the modern Visitor Centre (see photograph E142035, below). This ancient oak, completely hollow, is probably over 700 years old; it is now fenced off, and its heavy old boughs are propped up. It acquired its name not from its size or status, although it has a girth of about 33 feet (10 metres), but from Major Rooke, an antiquarian who described it in 1790. Before Major Rooke's interest the tree was known as the Queen Oak.

EDWINSTOWE, THE MAJOR OAK, SHERWOOD FOREST
c1965 E142035

CLUMBER PARK, HOUSE AND CHURCH FROM THE WEST
c1873 C500301

From the 18th century the great formal estates around Sherwood
Forest which were owned by four dukes, including the Dukes of
Newcastle and Portland, gave this area its nickname of the Dukeries.
One of these great ducal estates was Clumber, which was given
to the Duke of Newcastle in 1707. The mansion house shown in
photograph C500301 (above) was demolished in 1938, leaving the
18th- and 19th-century stable blocks, now used as the National Trust
Regional Office and visitors' centre. The Clumber spaniel takes its
name from Clumber Park, where the breed was first developed to
produce shooting dogs for the Dukes of Newcastle. The breeding is
unusual in that the dogs remain silent throughout the chase.

Newstead Abbey (an Augustinian priory founded in the 1160s) was dissolved by Henry VIII and granted to the Byron family in 1539. The house envelopes much of the cloisters and the buildings surrounding them, and the great 13th-century abbey west front survives. Newstead Abbey was inherited by the 'mad, bad and dangerous to know' poet Lord Byron in 1798, and he sold it in 1817. The house and its 300 acres of park were presented to the City of Nottingham in 1931, and major collections of Byron memorabilia were also given over the years,

LORD BYRON
1788-1824 A001087

which are displayed in the house. After Lord Byron's death in Greece in 1824 his body was brought back and buried in the family vault at Hucknall's parish church, four miles south of Newstead Abbey.

NEWSTEAD ABBEY, FROM THE WEST 1890 22856

Near the site of the priory church's high altar at Newstead Abbey, Lord Byron erected a splendid tomb to his beloved Newfoundland dog, Boatswain, who died in 1808 aged five (see photograph N29013, below). The inscription on the tomb reads:

'Near this spot are deposited the Remains of one Who possessed Beauty without Vanity, Strength without Insolence, Courage without Ferocity, and all the Virtues of Man without his Vices. This Praise, which would be unmeaning flattery if inscribed over Human Ashes, is but a just tribute to the Memory of Boatswain …'

Then follows a poem, with the last line:

'To mark a friend's remains these stones arise;
I never knew but one - and here he lies.'

NEWSTEAD ABBEY, BOATSWAIN THE DOG'S TOMB c1955 N29013

The area that is now Nottingham is believed to have been originally settled by the charmlessly-named 'Snot' or 'Snota'. Place-names ending in '-ingham' are usually names for early Anglo-Saxon settlements, and excavations have revealed evidence to back this up on the eastern of the two hills on which the city stands.

Cheapside in Nottingham, seen in photograph 22822 below, derived its name from the Old English word 'cepe', meaning bargain. Virtually everything seen in this photograph has been rebuilt since this view was taken. The fine range of buildings on the right, some medieval, and those including Smith's Shoe Booth which backed onto the old Exchange, were all swept away to make room for the much grander 1920s Council House building with its shopping arcades.

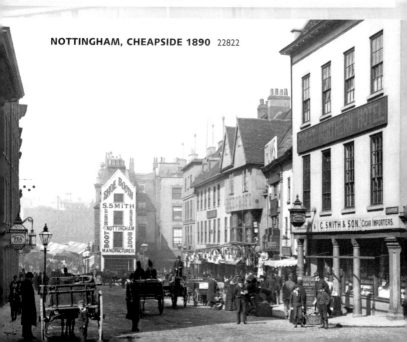

NOTTINGHAM, CHEAPSIDE 1890 22822

NOTTINGHAM, THE CASTLE 1890 22845

In the 14th and 15th centuries one of Nottingham's famous local industries was the carving of alabaster ornaments.

Following the Norman Conquest in 1066, William Peverel erected a castle on Tower Rock at Nottingham, a naturally impregnable site with towering cliffs on two sides. The castle dominated the country around, including the main road north, which crossed the River Trent below. From the mid 12th century it was an important royal castle, and in the 1470s it acquired grand state apartments in the middle bailey.

Several trades for which Nottingham was well known in the past are perpetuated by its street names, such as Pilcher Gate, named for the makers of 'pilchers', or furs, and Fletcher Gate, the street of 'fleshers' or butchers.

NOTTINGHAM, THE CASTLE GATEHOUSE 1920 69431

Beneath Nottingham's streets is a network of over 400 man-made caves, which visitors can explore on The Caves of Nottingham tour.

In the Middle Ages Nottingham prospered as a wool-dealing and cloth-making centre, and the River Trent was a vital trade artery. In the 18th century framework-knitting and bobbin lace took over, and these trades also spread to surrounding villages and towns. In later centuries Nottingham became famous for leather, textiles, engineering, tobacco, and bicycles. The innovatory tradition is continued by the University of Nottingham, which has been in the forefront of some of important developments of recent years, including the development of the first genetically modified tomato.

Charles I raised his standard at Nottingham Castle in 1642, the first action of the Civil War, although he soon left the town, which was strongly pro-Parliament. After the war the bulk of Nottingham's medieval castle was 'slighted', or rendered useless, by order of Parliament, and reduced to a ruin. Now only the outer bailey east walls and a 14th-century gatehouse survive, but the gatehouse was drastically restored in Victorian times, which unfortunately took away a lot of its character. A small amount of the original old stonework can be seen in the archway and at the foot of the right-hand tower in photograph 69431, opposite.

In the 17th century what remained of Nottingham's castle after the Civil War was given to the Duke of Newcastle, who had the upper and middle baileys cleared and levelled in order to build himself a ducal palace. The palace appears as austere as a prison block from a distance, but more ornamented when seen from a closer viewpoint. The building became a natural focus of resentment locally, and was sacked and burnt out during a riot in 1831, when Nottingham's outraged citizens learned that the Duke of Newcastle had voted against the Great Reform Bill. Eventually the ruin was taken over by the town and restored as a museum, which opened in 1878 as the first Museum of Fine Art in England outside London.

During the brief reign of Richard III, Nottingham Castle was the king's principal residence, and the great six-sided tower which he had built there was known as Richard's Tower. In 1484 while Richard and his queen, Anne, were at Nottingham Castle, they received the news that their only child, Edward, had died. The Croyland Chronicler recorded the reaction of the king and queen to the news in the following words: 'You might have seen the father and mother, after hearing the news at Nottingham where they were then staying, almost out of their minds for a long time when faced with the sudden grief'. Richard III referred to Nottingham Castle as his 'Castle of Care' (or 'grief') thereafter.

The famous Ye Olde Trip to Jerusalem Inn at Nottingham is claimed to be the oldest in England (see photograph N50041, below). It was reputedly founded in 1189 – this was the year when Richard the Lionheart began the Third Crusade, and legend has it that knights and travellers gathered here before their journey to Jerusalem, hence the inn's name. The present buildings are 17th-century at the earliest, with an 18th-century taller left bay. The inn incorporates cellars cut into the sandstone of Castle Hill, and it is possible that it was originally the brewhouse for Nottingham Castle – the brewing process requires a constant low temperature, which the caves provide; also, two 'chimneys' through the rock lead from the inn to the castle walls, which might have been used in the malting process, or to haul ale from the brewhouse up to the castle.

The Raleigh Cycle Company was founded in Nottingham by Frank Bowden, who in 1887 invested in a small bicycle works and within a few years had created the world's largest bicycle factory. James Samuel Archer, the co-inventor of the famous Sturmey-Archer three-speed bicycle gears, lived in Nottingham and worked at the Raleigh Cycle Company.

James Hargreaves introduced his 'Spinning Jenny' machine into a small spinning mill off Lower Parliament Street in Nottingham in 1767. Hargreaves was one of the founding fathers of the Industrial Revolution. His Spinning Jenny mechanised the spinning of yarn for weavers, speeding up the production process. Ironically, although his invention helped the mill-owners of Britain to achieve great wealth in the 18th and 19th centuries, James Hargreaves himself died in poverty in a Nottingham workhouse in 1777. In 1771 Richard Arkwright also set up his first spinning mill in Nottingham. These were both defining moments in the Industrial Revolution, but came at great cost to the cottage industry that already existed. The cottagers could not compete against the new machines in the industrial mills, and in desperation many of them banded together to destroy them. The gangs became known as Luddites, after their (probably imaginary) leader Ned Ludd. Although Luddism spread throughout the north of England during the early days of industrialisation, many people believe that the movement began in Nottingham.

(OPPOSITE PAGE) NOTTINGHAM, YE OLDE TRIP TO JERUSALEM INN 1949 N50041

Two of Nottingham's most successful entrepreneurs of the 19th century were Jesse Boot and John Player; the former developed a health empire, and the latter did his best to counter it by manufacturing billions of cigarettes! Jesse Boot, the founder of the chain of Boots the Chemist shops, started life in his widowed mother's herbalist shop on Goose Gate in Nottingham, and went on to found the Boot's Pure Drug Company in 1888. On the right of photograph 22823 (below) is Boots the Chemist's first shop, in Pelham Street in Nottingham, opened in 1892. There had been a small tobacco factory in Nottingham for over 50 years when John Player took it over in 1877, but it was in the late 1890s when the great expansion in the business took place which led in 1901 to the foundation of the Imperial Tobacco Company.

NOTTINGHAM, PELHAM STREET 1890 22823

A major part of Nottingham's heritage is its lace-making industry, remembered in the Lace Market area of the city, which in the 18th century was transformed from a residential area to a commercial capital. The industry was triggered by the development of two key inventions: in 1589 William Lee developed a framework knitting machine which enabled high volumes of lace to be manufactured, and in the 1800s John Heathcoate further developed this into a hand operated machine, allowing the industry to be mechanised. The industry was given a further boost with the introduction of steam power. Lace was extremely popular in the 19th century and early 20th centuries, in great demand as a symbol of both a well-dressed person and a home, and demand for Nottingham Lace was high – at one time over 130 lace-making factories were could be found in the Lace Market, along with offices and warehouses. The lace-making industry called for a variety of skills, from designing, manufacturing, bleaching, dying and finishing.

In 1910, H H Swinnerton recorded that the majority of the 25,000 people in Nottingham engaged in the lace-making industry were women, and described the lace-making process: 'A fancy lace does not come from the machine in single narrow strips as it is sold. A great many strips are made at once side by side. Their edges are held together by long threads running their whole length and they thus form a great sheet – a "piece" as it is termed – many yards long and several wide. The width of the piece, and therefore the number of strips in it, depends upon the length of the machine. In the earliest this was only 18 inches. In the newest, driven by steam or electric motor, it is as much as seven or eight yards. Whilst the lace is in the piece it is bleached, dyed, and finished. After this the strips have still to be set free one from another by drawing out the long threads. There are also numerous threads covering the lace which must be clipped away. Sometimes clipping frames are used, but both pieces of work are done mainly by hand and find employment for thousands of people in their own homes. It is a familiar sight in the side streets of Nottingham to see women sitting at the open door on a warm summer's day drawing, clipping, and scalloping lace.'
(From 'Cambridge County Geographies, Nottinghamshire', by H H Swinnerton, 1910)

Nottingham University started in the city in 1881 on South Sherwood Street. In the 1920s Jesse Boot, founder of Boots the Chemists, gave land to the west of Lenton, and University College moved here out of the city centre. Nottingham University College achieved independent university status in 1948; by then it stood in a park expanded from its original 60 acres to nearer 180 acres. The first building of the university in its new location was what is now known as the Trent Building (seen newly built in photograph 81570, below); it was begun in 1922 and opened in 1928 by George V, who immediately ennobled the generous Jesse Boot as Lord Trent. The lake and parkland setting was planned from the start.

William Booth, the founder of the Salvation Army, was born at 12 Notintone Place in Nottingham in 1829.

NOTTINGHAM, UNIVERSITY COLLEGE 1928 81570

Photograph 56562 (above) shows Nottingham's statue of Queen Victoria in its original position in Market Square in 1906. Unveiled amid great pomp in 1905, the year before this photograph was taken, Albert Toft's then-gleaming fresh marble statue was moved to the Memorial Gardens on Victoria Embankment in 1953, to make way for road widening. Its place has now been taken by a modern bronze family of four. In the foreground of this photograph a woman is choosing from the pots laid out on the Stones, the traditional site of the pot market, where goods were laid out on straw.

The recipe for the famous HP brown sauce was invented by a Nottingham shopkeeper, Frederick Gibson Garton. He called his sauce HP as he heard that it was being served in one of the restaurants in the Houses of Parliament. Unfortunately Mr Garton failed to make his fortune with HP sauce, as he sold the recipe and brand name for £150 to settle some debts.

Nottingham's famous Goose Fair, which for centuries was held in the Market Place, may have originally been held in Weekday Cross, and tradition states that it dates from 1284. The fair took place after harvest time, when the geese had been fattened on the corn stubble. The fair was originally intended as a market, but during the 20th century it became a pleasure fair that is held for three days every October. In its heyday as a hiring fair and autumn market for the Midlands it is estimated that up to 20,000 geese changed hands each year at the fair. A traditional way of cooking a roast goose in Nottingham is to rub the skin of the goose with salt and pepper and fill the cavity with a stuffing made of chopped cooking apples, sage and breadcrumbs. The skin should be pricked twice during the cooking to allow some of the excess fat to drain off, and give a crisp finish to the bird.

NOTTINGHAM, LONG ROW EAST 1902 48326

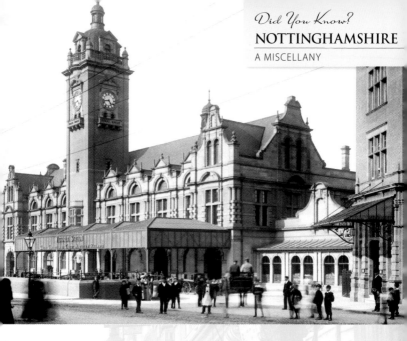

NOTTINGHAM, VICTORIA STATION 1902 48325

The Great Central Railway arrived in Nottingham in 1900 amid much fanfare, and its station, Victoria, cost a princely £1 million to build (see photograph 48325, above). The station was demolished to make way for the Victoria Centre in 1967, leaving only the tower intact as a sop to Nottingham's history.

Photograph 48326 (opposite) shows the Black Boy Hotel in Low Row, Nottingham in 1902. The flamboyant hotel was built in 1887 by the somewhat quirky Nottingham architect Watson Fothergill. Its lease expired in 1969 and its weirdly over-the-top architecture was swept away, to be replaced with a modern development. The flags in this view are flying to celebrate the end of the Boer War.

The River Trent is navigable for some 93 miles, and plays a vital role in linking the waterways of the North East with those of the Midlands. Before 1900, goods were trans-shipped to smaller boats at Newark: the river was only navigable from Trent Falls as far as the town, for beyond Newark it was fast-flowing and shallow, impassable for larger vessels bound for Nottingham. However, by the end of the Great War, the river was dredged to a minimum depth of five feet, and several locks were added. Nottingham was now less than a day's journey away from the port of Hull, which greatly increased its prosperity. In photograph 48328 (below) we can see A J Witty's pleasure steamers 'Sunbeam' and 'Queen' at Turney's Quay at Nottingham. River trips became so popular that a third vessel was required, the 'Empress', which was also built at Witty's boatyard. The 'Empress' was sunk in 1940 while on its second crossing to Dunkirk during the evacuation from France.

NOTTINGHAM, TRENT BRIDGE 1902 48328

Originally the main crossing of the River Trent from the south, the present elegant cast-iron Trent Bridge at Nottingham dates from 1871 and was designed by the Corporation Engineer, Marriott Ogle Tarbotton (see photograph 48328, below). It replaced the medieval bridge, which was in danger of collapsing. For a while the old and new bridges stood side by side, and for long after, Nottingham folk would talk of 'going down to the bridges'. By 1924 the increase in traffic necessitated the widening of the bridge and this was undertaken at a cost of £130,000. During the Second World War a temporary Bailey Bridge was stored for use in the event of Trent Bridge being bombed.

Stapleford, to the west of Nottingham and close to the Derbyshire border, is now virtually a satellite of Nottingham but grew up from a village of lace factories and framework knitters' houses. Its character is now that of a Victorian industrial town, but in Church Road there are some older houses and the parish church. St Helen's churchyard contains a great historical treasure – an Anglo-Saxon churchyard cross, the most important pre-Conquest monument in Nottinghamshire (on the extreme right of photograph S718026, below). Over ten feet high, with a protective hat-like capping of 1820, its date is uncertain but is probably 8th-century.

Nottinghamshire has its own variation of a raised pastry pie, similar to the Melton Mowbray Pie from neighbouring Leicestershire. However the Nottinghamshire pie does not contain pork, but is instead filled with gooseberries set in an apple jelly.

STAPLEFORD, THE CHURCH c1955 S718026

MANSFIELD, MARKET PLACE 1951 M184027

Mansfield lies some 14 miles north of Nottingham and to the west of Sherwood Forest. The centerpiece of the town's market place is the elaborate Gothic canopied memorial to Lord George Bentinck, politician son of the Duke of Portland, who died suddenly at Welbeck Abbey in 1848, shown in photograph M184027, above; funds for the project ran out, so there is no statue inside the monument. The pedimented building seen behind the Bentinck Memorial is the 1752 former Moot Hall given by Lady Oxford. All the buildings in this view survive more or less intact, and the Market Place is now largely pedestrianised.

The high quality Mansfield sandstone was quarried near the town and used widely – for example in the building of Newark Town Hall in the 1770s, as well as Mansfield's own Town Hall. Photograph M184024, below, shows Mansfield's once-famous rock dwellings, cut out of the sandstone, at Ratcliffe Gate. They were first mentioned in 1790, but are probably of much greater antiquity. They gradually fell out of use, and by 1894 only one was still recorded as being inhabited. They have now been entirely demolished on safety grounds.

MANSFIELD, ROCK DWELLING 1949 M184024

MISTERTON, THE CANAL LOCK
c1955 M235048

Throughout the northern part of Nottinghamshire the Chesterfield Canal can be seen – in Worksop, Retford, Misterton, and at its junction with the River Trent at West Stockwith, where a warehouse of 1789 survives. In Worksop, Pickford's Depository, an old warehouse, still survives, built in the early 19th century in yellow brick, and is now part of the Lock Tavern; it has trap doors for direct loading into the narrow barges, or 'cuckoos', as they were known, and a crane on the canal bank. The Chesterfield Canal, surveyed by the great canal builder James Brindley, took six years to complete, and opened in 1777. Built to carry coal to the Trent, it was taken over by a railway company in 1846, but it declined; the collapse of the Norwood Tunnel over the border in Yorkshire in 1908 effectively cut the canal in two. The canal ceased to be a trading route in the 20th century, and stretches were used for leisure. In 1961 enthusiasts formed the Chesterfield Canal Society, and the section through Nottinghamshire is now largely restored as a continuous route through the county, with all the locks fully functional. However, it is now almost solely used for leisure purposes, rather than commercial.

Eastwood is famous as the birthplace and home of the author D H Lawrence. Photograph E183004 (below) shows Nottingham Road, the principal shopping street, lined by mostly 19th-century buildings. To the left of the car, by the white-painted building, is the entrance to Victoria Street, where, in No 8a, D H Lawrence was born in 1885. The house, a two-up, two-down and attic, is now a museum which spreads into the shop next door, on the corner of the evocatively-named Scargill Street. The church spire in the distance is that of the Congregational chapel, where D H Lawrence first met Jessie Chambers of Haggs Farm, the 'Miriam' of his novel 'Sons and Lovers'; the church was demolished in the 1960s. It is a little ironic that the town that D H Lawrence offended so much by his book 'Sons and Lovers' now commemorates him, and even has a D H Lawrence Trail.

EASTWOOD, NOTTINGHAM ROAD 1955 E183004

FREEMAN HARDY & WILLIS

NEWARK-ON-TRENT, BRIDGE STREET 1906 56492

Newark-on-Trent grew up where the Fosse Way, the Roman road
from Axminster in Devon to Lincoln, met the medieval Great
North Road's predecessor and crossed the River Trent. The name is
Danish, meaning 'new fortress', and the strategic importance of the
river crossing defended by river cliffs is emphasised by Newark's
castle. The streets and lanes of the town are still mostly as laid out
by Alexander the Magnificent, Bishop of Lincoln in the early 12th
century. At the heart of Bishop Alexander's town was the large
market place into which the Fosse Way was diverted. Newark enjoyed
great prosperity in the 18th century through industrial growth and
through its status as a coaching town on the Great North Road.
There was much rebuilding then, so the town has a predominately
Georgian character; there was further rebuilding after the railway, the
east coast main line, arrived in the 1840s.

NEWARK-ON-TRENT, MARKET PLACE 1904 51736

Newark-on-Trent's beautifully-proportioned classical town hall of the 1770s is shown in photograph 51736 (above). It was designed by leading architect John Carr of York. Built in fine Mansfield sandstone, with an elegant pedimented and columned front, it incorporated a butchers' market, or 'shambles', behind, and is now converted into the Buttermarket shopping centre.

In the south-east corner of Newark-on-Trent's Market Square is Ye Olde White Hart, a superb and rich example of a late 15th-century timber framed building (see photograph N12006, below). Dilapidated for some years, it has now been beautifully restored, with the timber painted in many colours as an authentic reconstruction of a medieval colour scheme.

NEWARK-ON-TRENT, YE OLDE WHITE HART c1955 N12006

Stodman Street in Newark-on-Trent is where the famous Governor's House can be found, a 16th-century timber-framed house with three storeys of coved jetties (see photograph 61804, opposite). It has survived relatively unchanged because of its historical associations with the Civil War; it was the residence of Sir Richard Willis, the Royalist governor during the war, and a plaque informs us that King Charles I's nephew, the dashing cavalry leader Prince Rupert, stayed here in 1645.

The castle at Newark-on-Trent was started by Alexander, Bishop of Lincoln in the 1130s, but much of what we see now is 14th-century. King John died here in 1216, and in the Civil War of the 1640s the castle and town – which was staunchly Royalist – endured three long sieges. After the Civil War the castle was ordered to be demolished, but fortunately the long walls to the river front and half of the east wall largely survived. Newark-on-Trent withstood three sieges during the Civil War, in 1642, 1644 and 1646. Indeed, the town had extensive defensive earthworks all around it, with bastions for artillery pieces. Similarly, the besieging Parliamentarian forces threw up earthworks. Many of these remain, including The Queen's Sconce, an impressively complete earthwork battery in Devon Park; the Hawton Redoubt, south of the town; Sandhill Sconce; and others south of the Muskham Bridge. Such a complete picture of a 17th-century siege is very rare.

NEWARK-ON-TRENT, THE CASTLE 1923 74610

NEWARK-ON-TRENT, THE GOVERNOR'S OLD HOUSE 1909 61804

Six miles west of Newark-on-Trent is the small and delightful town of Southwell, whose minster church had been founded by the Archbishop of York before AD956. The Archbishop's Palace partly survives. The present minster church was begun c1108 and the Norman nave, transepts and west towers survive. The Norman east end was rebuilt later in the Middle Ages. Shown in photograph 24095 (below) are the Norman crossing tower, the north transept and the north porch. The minster became a cathedral in 1884. To the left of the photograph is the Chapter House of 1288, with its pointed roof. Built for Archbishop John de la Romaine, it is justly famed for the superb foliage carvings on its capitals and arches.

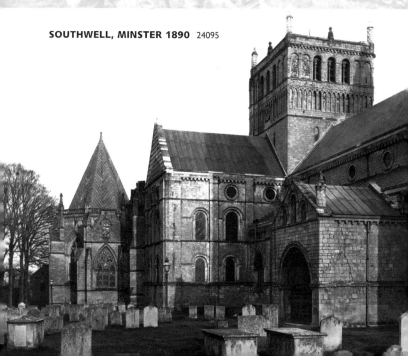

SOUTHWELL, MINSTER 1890 24095

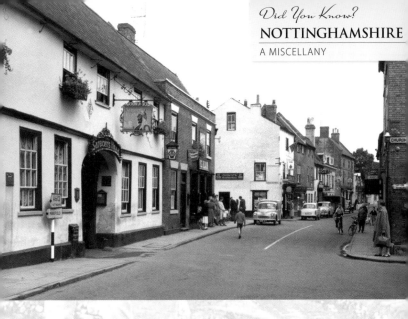

SOUTHWELL, MARKET PLACE c1960 S564026

Photograph S564026 (above) shows the Saracen's Head in Southwell, a 16th-century timber-framed inn in which during the Civil War, Charles I spent his last night of freedom in May 1646 before surrendering to the Scots and being handed over to Parliamentary forces (at that time it was known as the King's Head). Since this photograph was taken, the stucco which had been applied in 1693 to the first floor has been stripped off to reveal the timber-framing beneath.

WORKSOP, BRIDGE STREET c1965
W278025

WORKSOP, PRIORY CHURCH c1965 W278077

Worksop is the largest town in north Nottinghamshire, and is often seen as the gateway to the Dukeries. The town's finest building is the priory, formerly known as Radford Priory. The medieval town was at its gates, but moved northwards to its present location. The priory was founded c1120. The present nave dates from the later 12th century, and of the priory's east end only the superb Lady Chapel survives, The transepts with their two storeys of arches date from the 1920s and 1930s, while a modern central tower with a slender spire and a choir was erected from 1966 to 1974 by Laurence King. Of the priory buildings, only the mid 14th-century gatehouse survives, with the medieval market cross in front.

RETFORD, MARKET PLACE c1955 R261044

East Retford has at its heart a market place, first chartered in 1246. Since 1977 the market square has pedestrianised on non-market days, but until the A1 bypassed the town in the 1960s the Great North Road from London to Edinburgh streamed along its east side. Ironically, the old Great North Road had been diverted in 1766 so that East Retford could benefit economically from the coaching trade and commerce, while the Chesterfield Canal further boosted the town's prosperity, as did the coming of the railway in the 19th century. This prosperity was demonstrated in the building of a new Town Hall in the 1860s, seen in photograph R261044 (above) with its clock tower.

To the far north of Nottinghamshire the land is very flat, part of it including the Carrs, former marshes with vast skies of towering clouds, which were drained by Dutchmen in the 17th century. Drainage was not popular with the local population, as it robbed those villages on the marsh edge of their wildfowling and reed beds.

The cannon in East Retford's Cannon Square, seen in photograph R261028 (below), was captured at the battle of Sebastopol in 1855 during the Crimean War. During the Second World War the cannon and the distinctive iron railings around it were dismantled and stored for safe-keeping, and thus escaped being melted down as scrap metal for the war effort; both the cannon and the railings were reinstated in 1949.

RETFORD, CANNON SQUARE 1954 R261028

SUTTON-ON-TRENT, THE RIVER TRENT c1955 S236004

Low water levels during summer months often caused problems for barges on the River Trent, as seen in the 1950s photograph S236004, above. Over a dozen vessels heading upriver lie aground here, most built by Watsons of Gainsborough in the 1930s. The British Waterways Board then owned most of these craft and would usually send one of their tugs to work around the clock, trying to free the jam and keep the river traffic moving.

Holme is a hamlet on the east bank of the Trent slightly north of Winthorpe. The church was rebuilt in 1485 by John Barton of Calais. It is distinctive in that its porch, with its upper room and flanking round tower, would look more at home on a fortified manor house. The room above the porch is known as Nanny Scott's Chamber. The local legend is that during the Great Plague of the 1600s, one of the villagers, an old woman known as Nanny Scott, took refuge inside the room; eventually, having run out of food, she came out, only to find that all the other villagers had died except for just one man.

HOLME, ST GILES' CHURCH 1909 61810

SPORTING NOTTINGHAMSHIRE

The County Cricket Club at Trent Bridge was founded in 1841, but the grandstand, or pavilion, which still remains, was almost new when photograph 33250 (opposite) was taken. Six years later, on 1-3 June 1899, Trent Bridge staged its first test match between England and Australia. This was a particularly notable match, as not only was it the first game of the first ever 5-match series between the countries, but the England team was captained by the legendary W G Grace, who was playing his last England match at the grand old age (in cricketing terms) of 50 years and 320 days. Coincidentally, a player making his England debut in the same match, Wilfred Rhodes, was later to become the only other player to appear for England when over the age of 50. Trent Bridge is one of only five cricket grounds in the country where Test Matches are played.

A Nottinghamshire player – Wilfred Flowers – was the first cricket player to score a 'cricketer's double' – 100 wickets and 1,000 runs – in the 1883 season. Wilfred Flowers played for Nottinghamshire between 1877 and 1896, and played for England eight times, including two tours to Australia.

Mansfield-born Rebecca Adlington became Great Britain's most successful Olympic swimmer in 100 years when she won gold in both the 400m and the 800m women's freestyle event at the Beijing games in 2008.

November 1947 saw a football transfer which could surely never happen today. Tommy Lawton, one of the top players of the day, and an England international, joined Notts County FC for a British record fee, although County were in Division Three at the time. It was a sensational move, and caused over 45,000 people to attend the Boxing Day fixture against Swansea. Lawton is widely regarded as the best player ever to play for the club.

NOTTINGHAM, TRENT BRIDGE CRICKET GROUND 1893 33250

Nottingham Forest FC was born out of a group of players of a game called 'shinney', a popular 19th-century game similar to hockey. In 1865 the shinney players decided to form a football club, and Forest came into being. They called themselves 'Nottingham Forest' because they played on the Forest Recreation Ground. Their early years were marked by a number of 'firsts'. They were the first English team to wear shinguards. They also played in the first game where a referee's whistle was used. Most importantly from a football point of view, they are credited with inventing, under the leadership of Sam Widdowson, the classic football combination of the fullbacks, three halfbacks, and five forwards, the formation which was almost universal for more than 50 years.

Two football clubs have their grounds in or near Nottingham: Nottingham Forest, and Notts County, the oldest Football League club in the country.

Brian Clough OBE is regarded by many football fans as the greatest manager in the history of football, and has been referred to as 'the greatest manager England never had'. He managed Nottingham Forest FC from 1975 until 1993, and led the club to two European Cup wins, and two League championships. With characteristic modesty he once described himself thus: 'I wouldn't say I was the best manager in the business, but I was in the Top One.'

47

QUIZ QUESTIONS

Answers on page 52.

1. For some time in its history, Nottinghamshire was in a part of the country known as the 'Danelaw' – what was this?

2. In 1983 the ice skaters Jayne Torvill and Christopher Dean premiered their famous 'Bolero' routine at the British Championships at Nottingham. They went on to win the gold medal at the 1984 Sarajevo Winter Olympic Games with an unprecedented maximum score. What was the profession of Christopher Dean before he took up ice skating full time?

3. What ghastly event took place at Nottingham Castle in 1212?

4. He was born and bred in Nottingham; he began his football career with Arsenal; in his second season with Newcastle he scored 34 goals; on signing to Manchester United he broke the British transfer fee record, costing £6.25 million; he won the European 'Golden Boot' and PFA Young Player of the Year award in 1994; he has won Premier League, FA Cup and Champions League medals. Not bad for a Nottinghamshire boy! Who is he?

5. According to local legend, what was the reason that caused William Lee of Nottingham in 1685 to invent the framework knitting machine which revolutionised Nottingham's lacemaking industry?

6. In the 1970s a very important item of medical equipment was pioneered and developed at the University of Nottingham – what was it?

7. The village of Laxton in Nottinghamshire is a very special place for those interested in both history and agriculture – why is this?

8. The famous author D H Lawrence was born and brought up in Eastwood in Nottinghamshire. What was the occupation of his father?

9. By what complimentary name is Nottingham sometimes known?

10. What in Nottinghamshire was known in the past as 'The Key to the North'?

NOTTINGHAM, LONG ROW EAST 1890 22814

RECIPE

NOTTINGHAM GINGERBREAD

225g/8oz plain flour
4 level teaspoonfuls ground ginger
1 teaspoonful bicarbonate of soda
115g/4oz butter or margarine
115g/4oz soft brown sugar
115g/4oz golden syrup
115g/4oz black treacle
150ml/ ¼ pint milk
1 egg, beaten

Pre-heat the oven to 160°C/325°F/Gas Mark 3.

Grease an 18-20cm (7-8inch) square cake tin, and line the sides and bottom of the tin with greased greaseproof paper. Sieve together into a bowl the flour, ground ginger and bicarbonate of soda.

Place the butter or margarine, brown sugar, syrup, treacle and milk in a heavy-bottomed saucepan and melt it over a low heat, stirring continually. When everything has melted, remove the pan from the heat and allow the mixture to cool a little, then add the mixture to the dry ingredients, together with the beaten egg. Beat the mixture well for five minutes, until it is smooth and well combined. Pour the mixture into the prepared tin and level it evenly.

Cook in the pre-heated oven for about one hour, until the top is springy and the gingerbread is coming away from the sides of the tin. When cooked, turn out carefully onto a wire tray, remove the paper and allow to cool completely before cutting into squares, then store in an airtight container. This gingerbread should be stored for several days before eating, so that it becomes sticky.

RECIPE

NOTTINGHAM PUDDING

The Bramley cooking apple originates from Southwell, a small minster town a short distance from Nottingham, which holds an annual Bramley Apple Festival. The first tree grew from pips planted in her cottage garden in 1809 by a little girl called Mary Ann Brailsford; the cottage and garden was bought by a Southwell butcher, Matthew Bramley, in 1846, and ten years later a local nurseryman called Henry Merryweather asked permission to take cuttings from the apple tree to produce apple trees commercially – Bramley gave permission, but on condition that the apple from the trees should be named after him.

6 even-sized Bramley apples
75g/3oz butter
75g/3oz soft brown sugar
A pinch of ground nutmeg, to taste
A pinch of ground cinnamon, to taste
175g/6oz plain flour
A small amount of cold water
3 eggs, beaten
A pinch of salt
450ml/ ¾ pint milk

Pre-heat the oven to 200°C/400°F/Gas Mark 6

Peel and core the apples. Cream the butter and sugar together until light and fluffy, and add a good pinch each of nutmeg and cinnamon. Fill the centre of each apple with the mixture. Place the apples in a well-buttered ovenproof dish.

Blend the flour with a little cold water and add the well-beaten eggs to it, together with a pinch of salt and sufficient milk to make a thick, creamy batter. Pour the batter over the apples in the dish and bake in the pre-heated oven for 50 minutes.

QUIZ ANSWERS

1. At the Peace of Wedmore in AD878 between the invading Danes (or Vikings) and the Anglo-Saxon king, Alfred the Great, Nottinghamshire was absorbed into the 'Danelaw', the area of England which was to be under Danish control. Nottingham itself became one of the Danish 'Five Boroughs', along with Stamford, Leicester, Lincoln and nearby Derby. The period of Danish settlement and rule is remembered in the Danish place names which are common in the county, and include those ending in '-by', '-toft' and '-thorpe'.

2. Christopher Dean was formerly a policeman in Nottingham.

3. In 1212 King John hanged 28 Welsh boy hostages from Nottingham Castle walls during a Welsh rebellion.

4. Andy Cole.

5. The story says that he was courting a local girl who spent so much time knitting that he got the idea of inventing a mechanised knitting machine to allow them to spend more time together.

6. Magnetic resonance imaging scanners (known as MR scanners) were pioneered by Professor Peter Mansfield in the 1970s in the department of physics at the University of Nottingham. MR scanners are now used in hospitals throughout the world as a vital diagnostic tool. Professor Mansfield was knighted in recognition of his achievement, which has undoubtedly saved or prolonged thousands of lives.

7. The village of Laxton in Nottinghamshire is a very rare survival of the medieval open-field farming system that the 18th-century Enclosure Acts extinguished over most of England. Here, the village is surrounded by three great hedgeless fields, where crops are rotated and the fields are farmed in common. This remarkable survival of medieval practice is now carefully safeguarded and is a major feature of interest in the county.

8. D H Lawrence's father was a coal miner, and worked at the Brinsley Pit near Eastwood.

9. Nottingham is known by many as 'The Queen of the Midlands'.

10. In former times, the strategically important castle at Newark-on-Trent was known as 'The Key to the North'.

NOTTINGHAM, LONG ROW 1890 22815

FRANCIS FRITH

PIONEER VICTORIAN PHOTOGRAPHER

Francis Frith, founder of the world-famous photographic archive, was a complex and multi-talented man. A devout Quaker and a highly successful Victorian businessman, he was philosophical by nature and pioneering in outlook. By 1855 he had already established a wholesale grocery business in Liverpool, and sold it for the astonishing sum of £200,000, which is the equivalent today of over £15,000,000. Now in his thirties, and captivated by the new science of photography, Frith set out on a series of pioneering journeys up the Nile and to the Near East.

INTRIGUE AND EXPLORATION

He was the first photographer to venture beyond the sixth cataract of the Nile. Africa was still the mysterious 'Dark Continent', and Stanley and Livingstone's historic meeting was a decade into the future. The conditions for picture taking confound belief. He laboured for hours in his wicker dark-room in the sweltering heat of the desert, while the volatile chemicals fizzed dangerously in their trays. Back in London he exhibited his photographs and was 'rapturously cheered' by members of the Royal Society. His reputation as a photographer was made overnight.

VENTURE OF A LIFE-TIME

By the 1870s the railways had threaded their way across the country, and Bank Holidays and half-day Saturdays had been made obligatory by Act of Parliament. All of a sudden the working man and his family were able to enjoy days out, take holidays, and see a little more of the world.

With typical business acumen, Francis Frith foresaw that these new tourists would enjoy having souvenirs to commemorate their days out. For the next thirty years he travelled the country by train and by pony and trap, producing fine photographs of seaside resorts and beauty spots that were keenly bought by millions of Victorians. These prints were painstakingly pasted into family albums and pored over during the dark nights of winter, rekindling precious memories of summer excursions. Frith's studio was soon supplying retail shops all over the country, and by 1890 F Frith & Co had become the greatest specialist photographic publishing company in the world, with over 2,000 sales outlets, and pioneered the picture postcard.

FRANCIS FRITH'S LEGACY

Francis Frith had died in 1898 at his villa in Cannes, his great project still growing. By 1970 the archive he created contained over a third of a million pictures showing 7,000 British towns and villages.

Frith's legacy to us today is of immense significance and value, for the magnificent archive of evocative photographs he created provides a unique record of change in the cities, towns and villages throughout Britain over a century and more. Frith and his fellow studio photographers revisited locations many times down the years to update their views, compiling for us an enthralling and colourful pageant of British life and character.

We are fortunate that Frith was dedicated to recording the minutiae of everyday life. For it is this sheer wealth of visual data, the painstaking chronicle of changes in dress, transport, street layouts, buildings, housing and landscape that captivates us so much today, offering us a powerful link with the past and with the lives of our ancestors.

Computers have now made it possible for Frith's many thousands of images to be accessed almost instantly. The archive offers every one of us an opportunity to examine the places where we and our families have lived and worked down the years. Its images, depicting our shared past, are now bringing pleasure and enlightenment to millions around the world a century and more after his death.

For further information visit: www.francisfrith.com

INTERIOR DECORATION

Frith's photographs can be seen framed and as giant wall murals in thousands of pubs, restaurants, hotels, banks, retail stores and other public buildings throughout Britain. These provide interesting and attractive décor, generating strong local interest and acting as a powerful reminder of gentler days in our increasingly busy and frenetic world.

FRITH PRODUCTS

All Frith photographs are available as prints and posters in a variety of different sizes and styles. In the UK we also offer a range of other gift and stationery products illustrated with Frith photographs, although many of these are not available for delivery outside the UK – see our web site for more information on the products available for delivery in your country.

THE INTERNET

Over 100,000 photographs of Britain can be viewed and purchased on the Frith web site. The web site also includes memories and reminiscences contributed by our customers, who have personal knowledge of localities and of the people and properties depicted in Frith photographs. If you wish to learn more about a specific town or village you may find these reminiscences fascinating to browse. Why not add your own comments if you think they would be of interest to others? See **www.francisfrith.com**

PLEASE HELP US BRING FRITH'S PHOTOGRAPHS TO LIFE

Our authors do their best to recount the history of the places they write about. They give insights into how particular towns and villages developed, they describe the architecture of streets and buildings, and they discuss the lives of famous people who lived there. But however knowledgeable our authors are, the story they tell is necessarily incomplete.

Frith's photographs are so much more than plain historical documents. They are living proofs of the flow of human life down the generations. They show real people at real moments in history; and each of those people is the son or daughter of someone, the brother or sister, aunt or uncle, grandfather or grandmother of someone else. All of them lived, worked and played in the streets depicted in Frith's photographs.

We would be grateful if you would give us your insights into the places shown in our photographs: the streets and buildings, the shops, businesses and industries. Post your memories of life in those streets on the Frith website: what it was like growing up there, who ran the local shop and what shopping was like years ago; if your workplace is shown tell us about your working day and what the building is used for now. Read other visitors' memories and reconnect with your shared local history and heritage. With your help more and more Frith photographs can be brought to life, and vital memories preserved for posterity, and for the benefit of historians in the future.

Wherever possible, we will try to include some of your comments in future editions of our books. Moreover, if you spot errors in dates, titles or other facts, please let us know, because our archive records are not always completely accurate—they rely on 140 years of human endeavour and hand-compiled records. You can email us using the contact form on the website.

Thank you!

For further information, trade, or author enquiries
please contact us at the address below:

**The Francis Frith Collection, 6 Oakley Business Park,
Dinton, Salisbury, Wiltshire, England SP3 5EU.**
Tel: +44 (0)1722 716 376 Fax: +44 (0)1722 716 881
e-mail: sales@francisfrith.co.uk **www.francisfrith.com**